I0186288

Mixed Messages

The Erratic Poetry of John Cuetara

Mixed Messages © 2020 John Cuetara. All rights reserved. Big Table Publishing Company retains the right to reprint. Permission to reprint must be obtained from the author, who owns the copyright.

ISBN: 978-1-945917-63-9

Printed in the United States of America

Cover art: Edward Amado Cuetara
Digital Design by the Bytesized Studios, Christopher Reilley

Also by John Cuetara:

Other People's Problems
Other People's Bigger Problems
Away with Words

 BIG TABLE
Publishing

"Making other books jealous since 2004"

Big Table Publishing Company
Boston, MA and San Francisco, CA
www.bigtablepublishing.com

ACKNOWLEDGEMENTS

I want to thank my lovable wife Robin, who usually likes my poems, and my old pal Willie, who rarely does. I'm grateful to my muse Claudia and friends Anne, Donna, Sarah, Su, and Wendy for their highly constructive feedback. I'd also like to acknowledge my wise and funny editor/publisher, Robin Stratton of Big Table Publishing, for all her moral and technical support.

CONTENTS

Out West

I'd like to go back and rescue
the pill-taker, the nice girl
born by mistake to a drunken mother
and an angry father or vice versa
with hair as blond as Marilyn's.
We meet at a college party
with pot smoke so thick
she seems like a ghost
and later she sends lovely letters
from a ranch in Colorado
and writes poems
like Plath and Sexton's
hinting at what's to come.
Now I dream of searching
the mountains and finding her,
still young and beautiful,
under a pine tree
smiling.

Clean Mountains

Everything's purer in Vermont,
the snowy Green Mountains
with streams flowing down
their faces, the cheese and
ice cream from the milk
of local cows, the farmers,
artisans, even
politicians and when I
went to school there
I was purer too.

Good Legs

If I had two good legs
with strong calves and thighs
I'd never drive or ride the bus,
I'd walk for miles in every direction,
down cobblestone streets,
along windy white beaches
and into deep valleys just
to show off my perfect legs.
I'd climb the steepest hills
to make amends
with long lost friends.
I'd stroll through my mother's
garden cemetery, past the graves
of her famous neighbors,
sharing the news
and when it's all over
these two good legs are
what I'll miss the most.

Drinking Buddies

Drunk calling me
after midnight
like an old lover,
you recall the
golden boyhood
we never had,
naked swimming
at Walden,
that nice girl
from high school
we shared.
We've lost too much,
our youth and
dignity, and now
this stubborn
friendship is
drinking itself
to death.

Gypsy Brother

He was nothing like the dark
Romani men we saw in movies,
a blue-eyed boy heading west
in a caravan of one, sleeping by
quiet lakes, waking to the shouts
of locals chasing him off the land.
I wonder if he ever thinks about
the brothers who gave up on each
other years ago back in Boston.
These days truckers on western
highways know him better than I do,
an honest man with no plans
to settle down, no cards or crystal
ball to guide him, sitting by a campfire
strumming his guitar, unreachable
by fax or phone, hoping
to be left alone.

Everything

All I want for my boy
is everything I ever had
and everything I never had,
let him live among friends
in a peaceful place where
everyone's welcome,
console him when he
loses loved ones and
keep his arms, legs, heart
and brain working for
as long as he needs them.

A Wake All Night

You'd have loved this wake,
your children smiling like
tall statues, your pale wife
held up by sisters,
your devilish mustache
peering out from behind
a bouquet of roses,
the line of cheerful mourners
stretching around the corner
as though a mayor
or priest had died,
not just an average Joe.

Meeting Death

From my bicycle I see death
weaving down the road
in a black Mustang.
I'm riding past the lake
on a sunny spring day
thinking about flowers,
sailboats and pretty girls.
Death doesn't care
and swerves wildly,
nearly hitting me, then
pulls over by a lilac bush.
I see a shady figure
through the glass
and ride over to
introduce myself.

A Glorious Lack of Snow

It didn't snow last night
and I'm driving
through Cambridge
admiring the bare black
streets and clear sidewalks
of Harvard Square
watching sunshine
light up the slate roofs
of ancient Victorians
anticipating an easy climb
up my front steps
wondering why
anyone would want
to see such a
lovely old city
covered by snow.

For a Million

I'll happily return the million
to bring her back and hope
the siblings will give up theirs
though for that much we'll want
a guarantee she'll be around for
another five or ten years playing
the party games she loves
and hosting Thanksgivings
at the family home we'll
have to buy back from the
tech billionaires and we'll
all enjoy a few more snowy
Christmases at the lodge
in Waterville Valley
though none of us ski.

A Fearsome Love

I hold my fears tight like
my mother held her children
never favoring one over the others.
I fly through the clouds knowing
we'll all come crashing down together
like a carton of eggs and I could
talk for hours about the pain
of public speaking as the
crowd grows loud and blurry.
I'm always thinking about death,
the mother of all fears,
but deliver my mother's eulogy
from a pulpit high above the altar
without falling apart.

Dog Years

My dog-loving wife takes
great care of the furry old boy,
gives him a pep talk every
morning, brushes his teeth,
combs out his golden mane
and dispenses pain pills
buried in tasty liver snacks.
If she takes half as good care
of me I'll be happy, healthy
and well-groomed until I'm
six hundred in dog years.

Islanders

I see them clustered at
the ferry dock like seagulls
or driving their junkers
around this rock in Casco Bay,
crazy islanders who'll never
leave this familiar place
of weathered shingles,
grassy paths and craggy old
neighbors they love to hate.
I wish I could live here
in a cottage that smells
of pine and salt air,
surrounded by flowers,
but I can't spare the years
it takes to become
an islander.

Nothing to it

I don't have to do a thing
to keep this plane in the air
just relax and release the
armrests letting the pilot
fly us home to a safe piece
of ground somewhere and
I don't have to make the
the sun shine, the snow melt
or the flowers bloom
it just happens and I don't
have to run this fickle country
I'll leave that to bigger fools
and I don't have to prove
anything to anyone
and when it's over
dying won't be hard
as long as I don't
forget how to let go.

Snow Men

I'm waiting for the snow men
who always show up,
Dominicans toiling in
someone else's country
plowing someone else's snow,
husbands, brothers and sons
sending money home
to a steamy island.
I wake up sometimes on a
cold white night to find
teenagers shoveling my steps
and stand there watching
from inside my warm
house like a robber baron.
Some people don't want
them here, these short dark
men who work too hard
to worry about happiness,
but I'd be lost without them.

Your Father

I hear the news
after a week away by
listening to three messages
from my father's friend.
He says the weather's
been wild on the Vineyard,
high winds and flooding,
trees blown down, a real
rough spring and by the way,
your father's been sick,
then he says the weather's
improved but your father's
worse, it's pneumonia
and finally he says the
sun's come out, lilacs
are blooming and
I'm sorry to say
your father's died.

Home Visit

He sleeps in his childhood
bed on that last weekend
exploring old drawers
and bookcases.
He kicks a ball around in
the yard with the parents
laughing at the window
he broke years ago.
He rolls in the grass
with his boyhood dog
and pulls weeds from
the garden. He's a
good boy and they'll
miss him when
he goes.

Roadside Cowboy

The shirtless cowboy is waiting
for something to happen,
waiting by the roadside
with brown pectorals
and a felt hat
knowing that sooner or later
someone will stop,
a man, woman or teenager,
it doesn't matter,
a girl in a convertible
or a guy in a pick-up truck
will take him somewhere
a hundred miles west
or all the way to the coast,
he doesn't care.

Recoil

I've held a shiny pistol
in my hand,
black and poisonous,
felt it coil and recoil
like a hungry reptile,
watched it strike
and shred its prey.
I've killed in my sleep
and woken to regret it.
I've seen a black snake
sunning herself on
a rock knowing
she's going to kill.

Rites of Spring

Love washes up
on the beach with
eager waves and
sloshes back
into the sea.
Love's on its way
up in the elevator
at a Florida hotel.
It shines from
a thousand stars
as the children
of paradise fall
in love for a week.

Dark Beauty

I found a dark-haired
beauty from the past
selling real estate,
saying she's the
top seller in the city.
I remember dizzying
rides in her Spitfire and
drunken dinners with
the novelist
next door and now
these dark eyes
have bewitched me
into buying a house
I can't afford.

Beach Trip

We drive away
from the beach
with a mosquito
in our car
through traffic that
stops and starts
for no reason
only to have him
die a pointless death
miles from his
family and friends.

Past Lives

Let's go back and
be as thoughtful
as teenagers
can be, let's be
surprisingly nice
this time without
curses or slander.
Let's cling to sweet
memories through
the years and if
we can't do that
let's go back
and never meet.

Ancient History

Off to a rough start,
things lagged
in the middle
and ended poorly
but oh what a
time we had.

The Perfect Poet

You're working on the
perfect poem to make
us weep and smile,
the prize winner that
will change everything
assuring your place
among the greats.
You'll be the guest
of honor with so many
offers to publish,
teach, sleep around,
divorce and remarry
that you'll lose your mind
and become a great poet.

Happy as a House

Can a house make you happy?
Was it the furniture in the
old cottage, the wicker chairs
and saggy beds of my youth or
the things we played with in the
back yard, the hammock we rocked
with dizzying force or the shed
full of bikes and boogie boards?
Was it the women who ran the place,
Mom reading to us on the screened porch,
listening to the breakers rolling in
as Grandma, still alive at eighty-five,
leans over the stove stirring green
beans with onions and tomatoes?
These are the things that
made me happy.

Lost and Found

We lost a boy once,
a four-year-old blond
in a crowded crab shack,
a boy who proudly left
the table to find his own
way to the bathroom
and never returned.
Crazed parents searched
all the rest rooms, flushing
decorum down the toilet,
pounding on stall doors,
shouting his name, calling
managers and police until
he was found in the men's room
of a seafood place next door,
calmly drying his hands.

Waiting for a Ride

She waits in her
desert yard watching
for the spaceship
that will pick her up
and take her on a
heavenly adventure
like the boys did
when she was
young and fearless.

Street View

From where I sit
in a plastic chair
on the front lawn
this global pandemic
has a nice small-town feel
as mothers stroll by
with strollers smiling
from behind their masks
and a bare-faced jogger
huffs and puffs past me
with a guilty nod breathing
calmer air while
flowers bloom around us
and the birds and squirrels
throw a party in the yard.

An Unpleasant Person

I'm watching my sweet
mother's television
remembering how
she laughed at the
British sitcoms and how
seriously she took the
tragedies of Downton
Abbey in her final weeks.
I'm cursing an orange
charlatan on TV knowing
she wouldn't approve
as the meanest thing
she'd ever say about
someone is that he's
not a pleasant person.

Love in the Time of Corona

What's safe sex when
the virus is ringing our bells
and trying to slip inside
with the groceries,
when a kiss or even a
breath may be our last?
All that's left is love
through the wires,
a telephonic affair
in the dark,
a slow seduction alone
together listening for
sighs and zipper sounds,
undressing and
meaning it when
we moan into
the phone.

A Cruise to Nowhere

We're driving through ghost town/Boston,
the city of my birth, admiring the
empty silver buildings of the waterfront,
passing a lonely fleet of casino boats.
I'd like a lobster from one of these
shuttered seafood joints, I'd love to
take a booze cruise on that tour boat
or visit the modern art museum.
I'm ready to throw a party celebrating
spring and the end of hard times
like they did after World War II.
I love this old city and can't wait
for it to come back.

When I Lose it

I hope to lose it gradually,
gently, like a dithering old
aunt wandering off into
the woods at a family picnic,
wide-eyed and childish,
a distracted moth flittering
towards the light.
I want to laugh about places
and things I've forgotten
and live with people who are
growing milder not meaner.
I hope you'll visit and
if I can't remember
what we had together
let's assume it was love.

Goddess of Spring

Like Persephone
I want to take you away
for six months a year
to the southern underworld
where it's warm and wet
leaving the north to wither
and shiver without us.
We'll come rolling back in
late spring, brown and happy,
bringing sunshine, fruit and
flowers to a grateful land,
celebrating with friends
as though we'd
never left.

The Immortal Kennedys

We were playing basketball
in a neighbor's driveway
one dark November day
when a girl said
JFK's been shot.
The Kennedys were
everything to us,
brave, beautiful and cursed,
our robber barons
and our royalty,
they made us proud of
our little egg-head state.
They've been quiet lately
but I'm hoping they
can still save us.

To Do List

I want to take you to
an Italian restaurant
in the city serving
chianti in wine baskets
and declare my secret
love for you and
find a quiet place to
share the secret and
write a poem about us
which no one else
will ever read.

Unloved Child

There's nothing sadder
than the sound of a parent
and child not talking.
She's ungrateful, unreliable,
untamed, everything
you've made her.
She's turned them all
against you, family, friends
and even the squirrels
in your backyard
are on her side.
She speaks your language
so why not sit down
and talk to her.

A Fine Time for a Shrine

I've built a shrine with
pictures of my mother
hiking through the Rockies,
holding a koala in Australia
and wearing a long
blond wig at a party.
Her books fill my study,
her master's degree
sits on a lofty shelf,
her watercolor roses
hang in the kitchen
and her Tiffany lamp
brightens our bedroom.
If she could see the place
she'd smile as though this
was the most natural
thing in the world.

Laughter in the Bathroom

The redhead leaps
from my bed like a
flame, with flashes
of red and white,
dressing quickly
on this cold night.
Frigid air blows
through the
dorm room
as the door slams
with a curse.
I search the dark
hallways of my
conscience and find
her in a bathroom
brushing her teeth
with a gang of
laughing girls.

His Girls

He wants me to take care
of his dark-haired girls
if he doesn't make it
out of this hole.
He wants me to tell
them stories about
our early days driving
cabs through a crazy
city picking up celebrities
and drunks late at night.
I say I don't remember
so you better get well
and do it yourself.

Chicken Country

It's hot and wet
in the Mississippi town
where they kill chickens
for a living and cut
and package them.
The white women
worked here first,
then blacks,
slaving away for
minimum wage,
then came Latinos
but ICE took them away
and now the chickens
will just have to
kill themselves.

Dog and Country

My dog and I are falling apart,
a couple of old men in pain
taking Tramadol, damn it all,
struggling to get up the stairs
as our country falls apart.
He lies on the mat
waiting for treats,
hoping for a little ground
turkey or shredded cheese.
I watch the evening news
hoping the world won't end
tonight, knowing we should
turn off the TV and talk.
He watches me fill his bowl,
struggling to stand.
This may be our
last supper.

Motel Love

There are things we do
in motels that we never
do at home like watching
daytime TV in our underwear,
making love like lunatics
and swimming day and night.
It's a non-smoking world with
plenty of towels and friendly people
who smile from behind the desk.
We don't worry about noisy
neighbors who'll be gone tomorrow.
We drink water, soda or whiskey
with unlimited ice and dial zero
when things go wrong.
If pets were allowed
we'd stay forever.

Wasting Away

Like money,
time is most
enjoyable when
squandered so
I sleep late and
read bad novels
wasting away
on a distant beach
after summer's over
and everyone else
is back at work.

Family History

I'd like to apologize for
my racist relatives, red-faced
uncles smelling of sweat and
burnt rubber, who drove
big black Caddys through
their southern city years ago
shouting epithets and speeding
off into the hot hateful night.
I'm sorry for laughing at
jokes about people who
are invisible in the dark.
I know now that a rich
family history is no excuse.

The Light in her Eyes

Naked with you,
on you and in you,
we're two nudes
undressed for
the occasion
suddenly caught
in the bright lights
of her eyes.

I Confess

They're judging me
after I die, asking about
a girl I slept with at school
who killed herself, wondering
if I feel responsible.
We're holding hands on
a foggy field after a party
when she kisses me and asks,
at the moment of truth,
if I've been a good boy
or a bad boy and
I confess to being
an indifferent boy.

Lobster Shack

There's a place with a great salad bar
and a view of Portsmouth across the
Piscataqua where jolly waitresses
serve lobsters of all sizes and tell
jokes that make the world outside
seem brighter in any weather.
The walls and tables are cheery
pine and the room smells like
New England on a good day
and I can't imagine why
anyone would ever
want to leave.

Snow Mobile

He sleeps in his car
under four layers
of clothing as snow
falls on gas pumps
and golden arches
and dreams of the
family that used
to welcome him
so many months
or years ago.
He wakes to find
snow covering the
windows of his
cozy igloo.

Hiding in a Small Town

There's a town at the foot
of the Berkshires where
steep country roads smell
of smoke and melting snow,
a perfect place for hiding
from the law and other
big city problems.
He sits by the fire in
his white farm house
knowing the neighbors
will leave him alone.
No one notices the
quiet stranger who's been
hiding so long he can't
remember why.

Scavenger Hunt

Mother loved scavenger hunts
where partners searched
for objects in plain sight,
safety pins on curtains,
old postcards on dusty shelves
or paperclips on windowsills.
She stood over us smiling
down like God as we
ransacked the house.
She died years later
without telling us where
the money was hidden…
one last scavenger hunt.

Runaway

We ran from bullies and
parents, down driveways
and across back yards,
lungs aching in the cold,
telling everyone our
swiftness came from
wearing the right sneakers,
the fastest kids in the
toughest neighborhood,
chasing girls around the
public pool all summer
until I got hurt and they
ran on without me.

Circus Train

Love comes roaring in
like a train full of lions
and sets up a tent
in my small town.
Clowns in red wigs
and makeup jump
out of tiny cars.
My love walks tiptoe
across the high wire
knowing she'll never fall.

One Together

They work together
like teammates in a
three-legged race
helping each other
on the stairs.
They sit hunched over
the old roll top paying
bills for distant travels,
now distant memories.
She can't see and
he can't remember
but together they
perform everyday
miracles.

Cardinal Law

What kind of bird
is this lying on the
pavement like a
branch after a storm,
red as maple leaves
in fall, a cardinal or
red-faced warbler?
Was this an act of God
or a stealthy cat,
please tell me why
it had to end this way
on such a beautiful day.

With Elvis in Heaven

I'm burning with fever in
a hot little hospital room
as a priest murmurs in Latin
and a doctor tells me
to be a brave little boy.
I drift into a dream of
heaven with bright flowers,
sloping green lawns and a
white mansion like Graceland.
The angels wear white
jumpsuits and Elvis sings
softly from inside a cloud:
"Love me tender, love me
sweet, never let me go."
There's no pain up here
and everything makes
sense though none of it
matters anymore.

The Good Pain

The painful knot
slips down my leg
slowing me to the
pace of an old man
who sits at a table
in the garden watching
happy squirrels leap
from tree to tree.
I'm grateful for doctors
and druggists everywhere,
for a calm wife carrying
out milk and sandwiches
and for the September sun
shining its hopeful rays
on all of us.

Signs of Life

I've seen the signs online,
your name followed by R.I.P.
and no posts for months,
wondering if it's a prank
or something more serious.
Are you still out there
laughing at us,
casting wise cracks
in every direction?
Does your bleached hair
still sparkle in the sun?
Are you still cheering
the boys at the bar,
stroking their egos
and other parts?
Is there still time
for one more drink?

Someone Else's Bathroom

I see the pink sink
where she brushes her teeth
and washes her face and
imagine her womanly body
soaking in this tub
using products that smell
as sweet as she does.
Pill bottles peek out from
an open medicine cabinet,
antibiotics for mysterious
infections and valium to
soothe jangled nerves.
I've seen too much
and should leave
but I can't.

Sex in the Seventies

What a great decadent decade,
the age of disco when strippers
danced to Earth, Wind and Fire
and hard rockers rebelled.
These were my formative years,
strange times at a Vermont
college where students and
faculty shared wine and pot,
where I slept with girls who
smelled of patchouli oil
and a teacher took me
to his house in the woods
and fed me mushrooms.
I don't know why there was
so much sex in the seventies
and so little afterwards.

Crazy Love

Anything can happen
with your crazy love.
On nice days your lips
turn up in a wild smile
and we dance on the
beach in the sunshine.
On stormy days your
lips go down in a frown
and your eyes show
the wildcat inside.
Every morning I check
the weather to see
what kind of day
it will be.

Hothouse Flower

My mother called her
the hothouse flower,
this cruel and unusual girl
who lived with the ghosts
of her crazy parents,
saying and doing things
she'd regret in twenty years.
After this lovely flower was
plucked and began to wilt
she apologized for trespassing
against me and leading me
into temptation and I forgave
her as I hope they'll forgive
me for a lifetime of
bad thoughts.

Naked in the Dark

I'm half asleep
feeling the
bouncing of the bed,
hearing the rustling
of clothes coming
off in the dark,
wondering if
she's planning
to take a shower,
seduce me
or simply go
back to sleep
unencumbered.

Gift Baskets

My guilty conscience
makes me want to send gift
baskets to everyone I've hurt,
fancy ones with imported cheeses,
a big fat salami, mixed nuts,
a good bottle of wine, dried fruit
and gourmet cookies and crackers.
I'll start by sending them to
ex-girlfriends and siblings
then move on to former
friends and co-workers
and let's hope it makes
us all feel better.

Still Room

Light years away
a college on a hill
slips into the foggy past.
I open a familiar door and
step into a room that's
grown smaller over the years.
There's a tiny bed where
I slept with a red-haired girl
and windows looking out
on a mountain that turned
from green to orange to white.
The mountain is still there,
multicolored and huge,
and so are we though
the room no longer fits.

Subterranean Love

According to the writing
on my cellar wall
Cookie and Pierre were
lovers in May, 1970.
Was it just a downstairs affair
between a sweet local girl
and a French boy,
did Cookie crumble
when Pierre moved away
or are they married now
with sweet little things
of their own?

Heavenly Cats

From the highest pulpit
in a high Episcopal church
I'm looking down on
a sad crowd, telling them
about the calico cat you
loved and lost, how you
searched everywhere,
found the wrong cat,
took her home and
cherished her for years.
I say your heaven is filled
with cats and you're sitting
somewhere quiet now
surrounded by a sea of fur.

Same Old Wife and Son

If I had it to do over
I'd marry the same wife
and have the same son
but live in a warmer place
with more flowering trees
like Santa Barbara
where everything's new.
She'll swim in the ocean
all winter and he'll ride
his bike over brown
foothills to a better school
and we'll pity the poor
Bostonians shivering in
their historic homes.

Flying Away

Where are those people
who were once so important,
the dark-haired beauty who flew
away with my heart in her purse,
the restless brother who took
off in an RV years ago searching
for warm places and people,
the lost friend who flew off in
a rage vowing to forget us all?
In my dreams they're lying
together on a hot pacific
beach blaming me
for everything.

The End of the World

The beauty at the end of the world
is for lovers and losers,
for the joyous and wretched
and everyone in between.
I'm standing at the edge of
a steep green embankment
watching tall grass disappear
into a pine forest below.
As the sun sinks behind distant
mountains the mourning
dove's song reminds me of
everything that's gone wrong.
They say if you jump from
the end of the world
you'll disappear forever.

Ten Ordinary Sons

I'll sit down one dark
November day when
I'm very old and write
the boy a letter sharing
all the wisdom and advice
stored in my ancient brain
letting him know he was
loved more than any
ten ordinary sons then
I'll sail my old gray sloop
through all kinds of weather
towards some faraway island.

Magic Pools

Motels with magic pools
dot the East Coast
from Boston to Miami
breaking up the long trip
for a mother with squabbling
children heading south
in an old Ford wagon.
As the hot dirty sun sets
they leap into shallow water
splashing dangerously
close to the deep end
though none can swim.
The world underwater
is cool and blurry.
She laughs like a girl who's
never known trouble
inviting the children
to swim through her legs.

Two Apple Pies

I ran into you in
Harvard Square
years later
and you came
home with me
and baked two
delicious apple pies
and we ate
them both
and they were
better than sex
which always
fucks things up.

Memory Unit

She wonders when
she's leaving and
where her sister went.
The light from the TV shines
on her face revealing the
pale beauty of her youth.
As the sun sets behind
flowered curtains
a Caribbean angel asks
if she wants to go to bed.
She smiles and shrugs.
Aging beauties are parked
in every room of this
cheerful home where
everyone wants to leave.

The Last Coast

We're heading west on a Greyhound
following the path of earlier pioneers
picking up drifters along the way
letting the old life fade with the
years and miles as we pass through
desert towns with dusty cafes.
We barely remember the old house
covered with snow or the old friends
gathered at Christmastime.
The sun slips behind a mountain
dipping into an ocean we've never
seen a hundred miles west
in the promised land.

Boys and Men

There were problems
with the men in the family,
charmers who ran off
to foreign lands, drank
too much or moved
home with their mothers.
The wives lived long happy
lives without them, working
as teachers and nurses
and seeing the world,
leaving their sons to
wonder what it means
to be a man.

Stray Dogs and Girls

You're so much nicer
than the little wild beauty
who taught me about
sex in an empty mansion
that hot summer years ago.
Remember how she liked
the boys and what she
could make them do,
the fits of anger and affection,
the distracted parents and the
stray terrier she loved so much?
In the end she kept the dog
and gave me away.

Last Hours

They've left us alone
together in the wrong
room at the wrong time,
your sad sister and
two dark-haired boys.
Now I'm watching you
fade away, listening to
final words meant
for someone else,
wishing I'd known
you better.

Misplaced Affection

How careless
to lose a friend
so quickly with
a few slurred words,
drunken or stupid
generalities and
jokes I couldn't
take back.
I blame the hot
Spanish blood
of my ancestors.

Nobody

Nobody's kissing your cheek,
raking eager fingers
through your dark hair,
sighing into ears that
long for sweetness.
Nobody's admiring
your smooth white skin.
Nobody's touching
your active mind and
body though you wish
someone would.

Banks of the Mystic

Through my dentist's window
I watch a couple canoeing
down the Mystic River
as the laughing gas flows in
smelling of fresh flowers
they glide past the tavern
where "Jingle Bells" was composed
one drunken snowy night and
disappear under a stone bridge
as the river winds through
this stoic old city.

Lost Boy

You've disappeared
into a monastery with
the shaven head and white
robes of a Buddhist bride,
a skinny kid with a
joyful grin surviving on
brown rice and veggies.
Will you come see us in
the spring after hibernating
with the bears all winter?
You've found peace in the
Green Mountains but please
pity your poor parents
in the city of despair.

Passing Beauty

She stands on the
hillside looking over
a barren orchard
at colored mountains
in the distance
wondering where
the fruitful years went
recalling autumn days
picking apples with
shiny red cheeks
and selling them
to passing drivers
dazzled by the
beauty of nature.

A Heavy Door

I ask a friend what he needs
and he says write me a poem
so I wait in line for hours
outside the hospital room where
his daughter's saying goodbye
waiting in a white hallway
where friends stare at phones
hearing voices in the room
and in my head waiting
for the heavy door to open
waiting to read a poem.

The Sun's Pajamas

The children swim in a muddy cove
and slosh through the muck
feeling for clams with their feet
and on good nights when
nobody's drunk or fighting
they eat supper on the deck
watching the sun sink
slowly into the dark water
and don't go inside until
the mosquitos come out
and as they prepare for
bed their mother says
look the sun's putting
on its pajamas.

The Spaniard

We're flying over Asturias,
looking down at the wild wet
land where cows graze and
my grandfather was born.
To the east are the Cantabrian
Mountains where his Basque
ancestors fought off the French.
I only know him from the stories
my mother told, an old man
drunkenly cursing in Castilian,
passing meanness and
alcoholism down the line.
Years later we're visiting this
ragged green coast to see
where the trouble began.

What Comes with the Cottage

I remember the smell of
grandpa smoking cigars on
the screened porch as grandma
bakes chicken in the old cottage.
There's the screech of crickets
on a hot night and the whirring
of mourning doves in the afternoon,
there's the beach where we rode
huge waves, washing ashore
with seaweed and sand crabs
and those red-hot sunburns,
there are trips down the boardwalk
for ice cream and arcade games
in sneakers full of sand.
Should we hold onto these
memories or let them go
with the cottage?

Ghost Dog

We see our lovely blond
ghost dog everywhere
running across wet sand
on southern beaches at night
and crossing dark roads
with eyes gleaming
in the headlights
wondering why we
left him to fade out
in the arms of a stranger
while we suffer
silently in Savannah.

Intimates

I could sleep
in your bed for
months without
resorting to sex
as chaste as Gandhi
and his teenage girls
talking the night away
or silently reading
your mind.

Three Warnings

I'm lying here wondering
if I've learned anything
from mistakes I've made
over the years like
stealing desserts from
the school cafeteria
and getting fired for
insulting the boss and
driving into a rail yard
up onto the tracks
trying to find my
drunken way home
from a party laughing
with my sober
white-faced brother
by my side on our
last joyride together.
And I think the
answer is no.

Hidden Houses

The neighbors never
know whether they're
hearing shrieks of pain
or joy coming from the
house hidden by pines at
the end of a long driveway.
They're always surprised to
see the children running
around outside, red-faced
and disheveled, desperate
to play and never saying
what happens inside the
dark house though
I know because
I was there.

Smooth Operator

The girl appears out of
nowhere running me over
like a big beautiful bus
when I'm not looking.
We drive around with
her lovely friends
partying to the sweet
songs of Sade and just
as I'm feeling like the
coolest dude in school
the girl leaves me
humming to myself
by the side of a
sad highway.

Dreams of Marilyn

This beauty spent sad
days in a foster home
dreaming of movie stars.
She loses her keys
and wallet and worries
about losing her marbles.
With Marilyn's brilliant
hair and mind she
won't play dumb when
she meets the wrong man.
She plans to become
famous and I promise
to write a poem
about her.

The Man's Hands

He stands by the grave
apologizing through tears,
wishing he'd saved the man
years ago, feeling the
pressure of hands letting go
and hearing the screams.
He remembers kneeling
like a priest, pressing
rosary beads into a
limp palm, cradling
the wounded head,
saying "It's alright"
but knowing
it isn't.

Downriver

Her voice is weary
from making calls
selling software on a
hot July day while the
rest of the world's on
vacation and I'm stranded
in an office tower staring
out the window at
the little river below.
Take the afternoon off
and canoe with me, I say,
what's the worst that
could happen, a few hours
of uninterrupted peace
and quiet as we glide
downriver to the green sea,
catch the gulf stream
and drift away to
God knows where.

Old Neighbors

The TV glows in the dark
living room lighting
their white hair as
football players hop
around the field like
violent chess pieces.
He leans forward, ready
to spring from the bench,
while she dozes happily.
These stoic New Englanders
have lived here forever,
through sickness and surgeries,
cheerful and always
remembering birthdays,
never asking for anything.

Visiting Hours

I want to live in a bright
cheerful place with white walls,
sheets and towels, free from
noise and decisions where
I can wander through the
gardens thinking only of
lilacs and azaleas and you
can visit and see my lovely
watercolors but please
speak softly when meeting
my new friends and tell
everyone how happy
I am in this perfect place.

White Ferry

I'm searching for a soft landing,
considering the purple bed
of seaweed bobbing in the
waves as tall white caps and
bright patches of green
drift by on this hot day.
My only companions
the seagulls don't seem
concerned, shrugging
their black and white
shoulders in the sunshine.
Yearning for the cold water,
I slip over the rail, falling,
flying into sudsy seawater,
down, down into the
cool darkness,
floating up in time
to see the white ferry
steaming away.

Public Enemies

We've seen people
throwing whiskey bottles
from speeding cars and
running down squirrels
just for fun and now
we're watching them
take this country apart,
piece by piece, fouling
the air and corrupting
our government
until we're so angry
we want to burn
it all down.

Summers with your Father

Do you remember
when your old father
taught you to build
towering dribble castles
like cakes with white frosting
attracting children from
up and down the beach
and how he took you out in a
motorboat where you begged
to go farther, faster, Father,
past the breakers, beyond the islands
where he wouldn't go, afraid of
capsizing the ones he loved and
how he'd toss a ball with you
then sneak away to read
a book in the shade like
the old man he was.

A Flat State of Mind

An old man pedals past
neighbors in a shallow pool
as geckos climb the walls
and flowers wilt in the heat.
He nods to the men sweating
behind lawn mowers
and dreams of escaping
the Sunshine State,
riding north past a thousand
gated communities until
the air turns cool.
He thinks about snow
and remembers building
an igloo with his son
and huddling together
in the darkness.
He wants to call the boy
but doesn't know
what to say.

Boy in a Box

The substitute startles
hearing her eighth graders
talking to a box, telling it jokes,
making laughter pour out
of its gray metal sides.
They call the thing Johnny,
discussing sports and
homework he'll never do.
Nobody tells her about
the boy at the other
end of the intercom,
miles away in a hospital,
who may or may not
be coming back.

www.ingramcontent.com/pod-product-compliance
Lightning Source LLC
Chambersburg PA
CBHW020945090426
42736CB00010B/1265